Whatever Speaks on Behalf of Hashish

Whatever Speaks on Behalf of Hashish

Poems
by Anis Shivani

BLAZEVOX[BOOKS]

Buffalo, New York

Interior design and typesetting by Geoffrey Gatza
Cover Art: Heinrich Vogeler, *The Island of Peace*, ca. 1918-1919, oil on canvas, 41 1/8 x 38 in.
Courtesy of the Yale University Art Gallery.
Illustrations: The illustrations are all images of woodcuts by Ernst Ludwig Kirchner, part of the
collection at the Robert Gore Rifkind Center for German Expressionist Studies at the Los Angeles
County Museum of Art, and are reproduced here courtesy of the museum.

First Edition
ISBN: 978-1-60964-227-3
Library of Congress Control Number: 2015948504

BlazeVOX [books]
131 Euclid Ave
Kenmore, NY 14217

Editor@blazevox.org

publisher of weird little books

BlazeVOX [books]

blazevox.org

21 20 19 18 17 16 15 14 13 12 01 02 03 04 05 06 07 08 09 10

For Mehnaaz

Table of Contents

V.

VI.

VII.

Acknowledgments

About Place Journal: "Elm"

The Baffler: "Without Which He Would Not Have Written His Best Poems"

Blackbird: "Translations from Lorca"

Boulevard: "Sonnets to X."

Drunken Boat: "Ars Poetica," "Bookseller," and "Objects"

Epoch: "the death of frank o'hara"

Interim: "Confessions" and "Dear Foucault"

Green Mountains Review: "Sonnets to X."

The Missing Slate: "Alexandria in World War II"

Pank: "Conjunctivitis"

The Portland Review: "December 31"

Scud: "Cat," "Man with the Movie Camera," and "War"

Verse: "Autobiography of a Graffiti Villain"

"Controlled Demolition" appears in the anthology *Devouring the Green: Fear of a Human Planet* (Jaded Ibis Press, 2015), for which I think editors Sam Witt and Debra Di Blasi.

Thanks above all to Geoffrey Gatza for his editorial courage and vision, and for publishing this book.

Illumination

We hurt the piano's backbone, we revert to the nuisance of commuters on ischemic trains. Fate, a novitiate marker of swollen blue feet in the petite morgue. Do you believe in turtles shedding light? I was in a hammock, stranded in threads of sun, numberless. One should welcome the positively dynamic chairs whose unseen thorns we inhabit in a cerulean morning of surpassing ceremony, whereafter we proceed to the seminar of abstraction where écriture féminine occurs at last to the shifting glances of open windows. Acrostic, make water heavy, turn in your canceled checks: lavish with cartons of cigars, fine wines beloved of the caricatures of bestiality, trombones splashing out a migraine of obsessive love, feet that got burnt at South Beach when no one was looking. Everyone falls in love with their own wrong side. I will let you through, this one time, but there is the broken turnstile, do you see the angry morning come to a crest? Pornography is nothing if not the febrile curves of the sun in decline. Or I should say a possibility of kidnapping, and the nose, curmudgeonly all through the fascist years, is suddenly a delicate instrument of joy. This is a television of bankruptcy. I am not getting through to you, it is impossible when you are listening so intently. If you had been a spectator at the Black Death, you would have been surprised at the sheer amount of noise: nostalgia for things unknown, unseen, for the row of poets who stand condemned by the arsenals of democracy, their bald heads itching from the tortures of summer. If you come to me in the best hours of the night, but you never do… After the death of the fly all noise ceases. The quiet extends from the beginning of human history until the end. The age of the worker becomes opaque through unequal tempo. To have been Lorca in the moment of surprise! To have descended into Granada on the wings of sturdy morality, forever immune to petty thievery! For being queer. For being a waffler. For the hyperbole of folklore. What can I say about you that's new? Montaigne thought it a matter of thinking things out, like a porn star in retirement, looking back over the ups and downs of a career of entente. The clerk in me clinches the argument through muscle strain. The sound of the sparkling souvenir, supplement to human rights, every chalky supper changing me imperceptibly into chamber music, a conscript outfitted for originality. Pest, your perversions are insignia for rocks metamorphosed into black squirrels, agouti, pocket gophers, the too soft colors of socialists in sitting rooms.

I.

December 31

bernadette mayer
how did you live through the bush years
i didn't win any prizes
but winter surprised like a second childhood
to the tenebrous nursery a decade late
wolf spoor kept woman awake
in the far cabin
snowy light falling mute
to the clomp of the bearish
moon oh it's been all right
i know my length in meters
i have my magic marker
and you your forest
this line makes it a sonnet

the death of frank o'hara

came like shampoo on coconuts, or no,
i meant like a laughtrack lost on the moon's
gravityless surface, everyone leaped aside,
frank! frank! the dune buggy, fender sticking out,
like a gunman's silent gesture, hand in pocket,
or no, out there where the moon hits it in silver
coin, mangling the liver, poor frank's already
dying liver, or no, not dead yet just damaged,
which is to say days and nights of hallucination,
grace, jane, bunny, i am talking fast now,
faster and faster, this is what happens at death,
at last all my inhibitions are at rest, or no,
it is like this disco summer on fire island testing
arbitrageurs' souls, riffing off the city's parlor
games of art and art worship and worship of crudeness,
in man-woman embrace, or no, limp penis to penis,
john, ken, bill, this is what happens at death,
at last i've become a surrealist hit by sense.

Dear Kenneth Koch

my street of poets (pink crevasse) tumid volcano
firing jets of lyrics on Sunday afternoons
when i put you aside, kenneth, eager
to entrail caesuras from your thousandth
unknown play, for barbies doused
in gasoline, yes, that's the metaphor i want
to steal from your snail of a bed,
virgin oaks dying suddenly in my yard
on the very day i check
microscopes for efficiency

Averroes

1.

Ahead of the moving company, whar your gwine,
aha, said Adam, my God I warm myself and our eye
has seen it. But the stomach, when shall all men good
be sudden fits of ague, now the mighty Centaur seems
to lead: the astronaut is going to find he was only
twenty dolphins ahead, sheer Africanity, aformosia
in common with consumer's paradise of transistors,
food mixers, and but a faint struggle with servants.
If you look out my window at the superlatives of haze,
thrice does she sink down in deadly snows: all foods
are out of their wits, alleged rocks or minerals, yet
you draw not iron, not rhetorical names, but Adam's
style—my governor this morning, colonist of interests
as old as hydrocarbon, things intended to be heard.
To what is to be attributed the extinction of the mystic
orgies of the East? Grown together by adhesion of
voyages, under stones, dead leaves, eruption of fine
arts, abstinent bridegrooms, two of whom were cur-
tailed in the handles. Cross a pike, water, provision
of epitome; representation of some parts of plaintiff's
demands; abrasive on the sea bed; the place where I
stop; seamen and carpenters employed all night to take
the average of opinions—into which we return at death.

2.

Au pair yielding gold, ask aunty to come and cut it
for me, sometimes with the idea of instrumentality.
I have arisen to vigor, heroic aspiring, careless rage,
the eastern languages failing to express the vowels.
Why chew leathery beef in the aspidistral bliss, the
weed of life grows where air is hot and winnowed.
Machines of ostentation, a wooden beam, a missile
on land, on board ship, thus apocalyptic visions are
made to seem very trim and express: this polluted
chancellor, horrid blasphemer, another system of
telling fortunes, present in pure arithmetic. Bare-
footed predestination, bohemians at the Parthenon,
the alks built upon rocks, it was a cold dagger au
naturel. The likeness of stone weight you've seen
in the literature of amputation, whenever surfaces
become sore. By attrition of ceremony, the kindle
flames around the solar disk; practically every man
is an atheist, heir apparent to the throne. Sufferings
which fit me for future happiness, hang no weight
upon my heart, the design afterwards used as flag.

3.

Or quiet, busied in appeasing, grim appearance in
your favor, all the lines represent judges like the
lesser sort of birds' eggs—a phantom or apparition
to secure worldwide political appeasement. The
apartment has an elevator. These foolish things, a
tinkling piano, your phosphate of lime, animals
mimicking human form, ten days' ration should the
moment come. There would be the semblance of a
general retreat from the apex. Can you ante up?
You pay as you enter, you whose business is to walk
in front, as an usher, an ant-eater, a bird of gray
plumage, the axle-tree of the antarctic. Lantern of
subtleties, I want arithmetic: sequence of numbers
in which popes power aristocracies of reason and
virtue. If she would apply to his request, she would
be set to liberty. A death's head grins like an antic,
behind this drum are several vaults, hybrids, macro-
scopes, humiliation of fractured limbs. The double-
mindednes of the word "dux," burlesque writing
filled with nonsense, brave assassins stabbing in the
dark: this house is restored of hearth, of astral lamps.

dear foucault

imitation of discourse
twin trips to harmony gendered firewalls
water she said gurgling along canals
of intestines bees-worlds duped in
nephrous sentences balloon-like
sun-diagram in ruffian drums pinned
internet grapes yagodas bluish
and believable eyes
of butterblue taffeta
mimicry of unseatable guests

Three Poems After Po Chü-i

Bookcase

Once assembled, it keeps challenging me day and night
as though I needed to learn the names of useful officials.
I want metaphysics to be a rounded number, a fitted jacket,
I want my friends not to worry about the lost caskets of wine.

Bird

When parents die, children often fall in love with given names.
They are like holiday bells, jangling happiness long after sunset.
You hop on my palm, tickling me, stretching your tiny beak,
and I extract grain after grain from my pocket, teasing you.

China

My lover claims her poet grandfather, a true man of the people,
lavished care on servants, a patriarch who was rightly mourned.
It is he who believed in food as magic, inviting enemies over,
trusting each morsel would burn its way to their waxing hearts.

Gertrude Stein

The sash is not like anything mustard
Called to the telephone six times during this effort

If lilies are lily white if they exhaust noise
Horseshoe nails, pebbles, pipe-type cigarette holders

A blue coat is guided guided away
As stupid, as barbaric as successful barbarism demands

If the speed is open, if the color is careless
I've done some discovering and some propaganda

A color in shaving, a saloon is well placed
Fingernails which, daily, she trimmed and polished

A winning of all the blessings, a sample not a sample
Paragraphs are emotional, sentences are not

Cough out cough out in the leather and really feather
Since her time, oily tides of kitsch have continued

A shawl is a wedding, a piece of wax
Ridiculous miniature alabaster fountains

Dear Colm Tóibín

Except, in Barcelona,
I've heard Franco's ghost still haunts
the middle streets
in search of noumena
flattening the illicit
lovers' first glimpse of morning
with rows of corpses near
as the eyelid, so you can feel
the last breaths of your compatriots
hurrying out,
lusting to leave the gossip-city.

II.

Sonnets to X.

1.

You believed in easy cults, houses of worship,
plain Janes retrofitted to curl their unsightly toes
in bags of guilt, every Rama a guru, every
guru an ocean of passion, every neighbor
a quest for perfection. Those boxcars got off
the rails once, and the fixers fixated on piles
of rubble hiding gold in plain sight—who knew
black markets were born in burning daylight?
As for me, I wasted my Zarathustra on you,
I planted the seeds of decadence in soil both
aspersive and reflexive—mirror, O hurt mirror!—
and became fatigued and cross, watching you
absorb my lessons like an adept secretary,
when I wanted the sinister abbess of my dreams.

2.

Once we were comparing notes on the Egypt of
fancy, and thought Durrell was way off mark.
In Alexandria, prostitutes are really rabbis and
small-hearted rabble in mourning: give them
the right of way, let them talk themselves into jails
and dungeons, the black seas dribbling biblically
past nude forks in history. As we know, colonialism
was a matter of giving the educated folk their
bright insignia, names of live philosophers, gifts
of precious animals, identification with kings.
This Berryman who wrote sonnets for you—how
many brooding ill-starred gypsies are there in a
single universe?—knew how to divide and conquer,
but I am no match for his mockery of your story.

3.

Was it all right to burn the house in California?
We escaped in the dead of night to Vegas, drunk
on the cosmic prank that brings contenders together,
caught in limbo, in paradise-on-stilts, until either
the sea evaporates or the desert blooms, until
Bukowski himself emerges from drug rehab,
and Anaïs Nin offers to enter the monastery.
No, our house was an effrontery to poetry,
don't you see? Guests were always losing
their only copies of manuscripts, neighbors'
kids turned lifelong enemies of the state,
pets died, old-timers fucked like teenagers.
Out here, the road stretches like a severed limb,
the only thing detaining us a moon behind fog.

4.

O no, you misrepresent *Le Mepris*, not Bardot,
not Piccoli, not Godard, but Moravia we must
blame. You bracket hypothetical love in sonnets
of treachery. After suspicion, jealousy, bitterness,
revenge, and malice, only the wide flight of fancy
in blue-lettered Capri, home of the *Odyssey*, stirs
justice. Only if love is death is everyone blame-
less. Films are silent bullhorns, rascally friends
wrecking our doppelgänger. On another note.
I will gift you Wilkie Collins's paranoid chair.
I will ambush the vanities of philanthropy.
I will teach you Greek in two months, French in three.
There are not enough languages to erase your cool,
not enough colorful styles in which to die.

5.

My love, you will not survive, I guarantee,
the immigrant's rigors of truth and lies.
Calculations of mortifications best delayed.
You are a flower I painted in a sideways dream.
There is hope for me, if I can jump the fence.
Freeway of death, cars sundered like rabbits.
You want to know the truth, nothing but the.
I left my wallet buried in the sand, under an
African plantation sun. Henry James can never
be my brother. You tutor the blind and dumb.
I read all the books worth reading in the womb.
An immigrant is an explosion waiting to happen.
You want me to count the ways I love you?
Fraulein X., I am black chalk in a Berlin cave.

6.

It is time for false images to be put aside.
What does that mean, O Beatrice of millennia-
pressed-into-putty, how may we provide
a free puppet show to partisans of love
and philosophy alike, without committing
to either side? I will not want to have visions
of your death scene, gracious ladies or no.
I think you were my screen lady to begin with,
letting me see erosion of layers of history humped
into short stumps of color, a painted desert.
Beside you is a circle of protective friends,
who cry at my smallest handkerchief error,
who perceive me as the worst poet in the land,
and I've given them no reason to think otherwise.

7.

The years of plague came and went: something
like art for art's sake. Dried pustules were granted
to the luckiest, warm corpses inhabited castles
of humiliation run by doctors of philosophy.
Dante ran away, and Swift, and Dr. Johnson.
Left behind were cities of crime, cities of passion.
Walls were graffitied with the antithesis of your
polite name, in the news childkillers were praised
for their perspicuous sense, their prior illumination.
Art for art's sake is a cycle of genetic defects
at last run its course—the warm fist of history
blackening its own face. You took first place.
All the years of waiting for you to catch up,
and I still can't find the keys, still have no door.

8.

O gracious Beatrice, who sullied my ferocious
indignation when you compared me to a mortal,
why did you shun the greeting when I needed it
most? We'll let bygones be bygones, although
in the literature between our two sides, it seems
one-upmanship has been the rule. In another
time I might have taken the cross, worshiped
secular authority, sailed to Constantinople rich
in self-belief. X. is a dagger I run my finger
along every morning, wondering should I at last
kill myself? But honesty prevents martyrdom.
At nine, already my eyes were luminescent
with the grief of mortality, knowing your end
would be unnoticed, like birds fading in crowds.

9.

We've been fighting over Ezra Pound all along.
One way to love is to bend the will like a broken
arm, twist it in the forbidden direction, broadcast
the victory of weak armies in poetry's badlands.
Madman or savant, naïf or sage, your enemy or
my protector? Another way to love is to sublimate
anger and hatred into newness for nothing's sake,
leach the color out of the white sand, encrust in
marble the manic urge to record our minds copulate.
Ezra, congregating around himself at St. Elizabeths,
poets with rocks in their pockets, tigers for brains.
One of us has to kill him, for this love to go on.
We cannot linger in this limbo, your chaste hair
is beginning to scream at me for a scene of violence.

10.

Which side of Cavafy shall we wake up on?
Your beloved Alexandrian gentleman is paying
centuries-old dues to patrons of the talking
arts, using one side of the brain, stopping short
of the threshold of consciousness. How he leads
us on wild-goose chases through aristocracy's
rain-house of fragile knowledge! To join victory
parades, every cell of the erotic being must rank
the beginnings of nations, when ornate nebulae
clouded direct calculus, and the poor passed
without trouble. Do you really want that life?
You would stand at water's edge, indifferent
to the sweeping gulls, shining like a million
dollars, unattainable by thieves like me.

11.

Yes, Alexandria, the gentleman in the white suit
standing at a slight angle to the universe could be
me, if I'd had the right education in the classics,
if I'd had beloved Antioch or some similar quake-
destroyed ancient town for attachment, if cafes
in the declining parts of town were where I held
court, ennobling the night's hard crust of love.
I would be immobilized like a bird caught in fire.
But this is not me. Your eroticism is an unmixed
message, as is always the case with well-fed girls,
you have never betrayed the brutal singularity,
you believe in reincarnation, coming back to
avenge every dream, and the damp pelts of hurt
on your back are in fact signs of harmless peeves.

12.

Enough, this sod-burned Europe of Rilke, banned
to publicists of love, permitting nymphic lust only
in stone-cold castles; enough, this ferny mind-
field of a dead Europe where lovers circulate
in the stables of intimacies like so many chaste
vampires, where no transgression is finally
of consequence; enough of the deathbed
correspondences, shunning the last prayers
of illegitimate children legitimated by fame,
the only glue binding princesses and commoners.
Where is the skill to crunch horoscopes of death
in a single injured hand, write oneself out of
chronicles of protest? Rilke would have given up,
at earliest dawn, your scroll of wise sayings.

13.

We were searching for Sappho's academy
on the carefree island of Lesbos. It is best
to survive in fragments, I said, if you live
by the lyre. You insisted she jumped off a
cliff in love with the ferryman. Was Cleis
her daughter or lover, and does it matter?
Nine times fate called and she rose like
Socrates to take all the questions and refute
none. It matters that you are of her party—
when all is said and done. I think centuries
ahead, as my race is said to do, I am yellow-
backed and cavelike when I research my
own past. You, like Sappho, decline to state
the plain truth—that my days are numbered.

14.

O Sappho, academician of wholesome truth,
widow of lyricism, patron of daughters who
merged into lovers who merged into mothers,
one of the nine who resembled the Gods,
the world has been waiting for you to appear
in some new guise, but you have disappointed.
The fragments alone are unbearably solid.
Is it true the girls flocked to your island only to
drown in flasks of ecstasy, while you entered
their burnished names in the registry of eros?
The world has been waiting for you to appear.
Would you accept us in your academy, X. and
I, give us new names, point out the ferryman
for whom you were said to have drowned?

15.

There sat Adam Zagajewski, chewing the
matter of Poland, all those years ago, at Brazos
on one of those hot Texas days when
nothing moves, except the puppets of
history. It has already been fifteen years,
while he has only grown younger, as the
greatest poets do, he has managed to outdo
every tyrant of his time, he has silenced
every dark critic, painted his own aura in hues
of gold, single-mindedly god-forgiven and
angelic in how he manages to calm non-
existent fears. He was besotted by your
long legs and fearless eyes, he said he would
give up all of history to spend a day with you.

III.

A Dream of Burial

After James Wright

First my head, repository of welcomes.
In misordered sequence, torso like crows

torn apart by sulphur, hands misshaped
like lionesses' manes, a horse's genitals

where they least count, in the workhouse
of war. I am a page of god's true honey

viewed like this. Or a feeble nasturtium.
All things are embodied in silent fingers,

crotchety like the doors of afternoon.

Recluse

1.

Cyclamen, sundew, purple sarsaparilla, and the
scarlet pea, on the hill beautiful sarcenet skirts
are edged with flamy gold: sudden demand for
long white gloves, the Babylonian name for the
year 3,600 in the surrounding villages. Lunar
eclipses repeat themselves. Within an hour
people clamor for tea and sarnies, but I'm funny
where dope is concerned. Actors be released
from polo practice! We had a tape playing of
sarod music, climbing arms, a craftsman to take
the matter up, a gallant show in hoops, patches,
lace, and muslin. You bestir yourself full of
your own wool sentences, paper to wrap fire,
wrapper of culture and the sea-robin, a century
of the encyclopedic toadfish. Groin deep the man
in me has the advantage. The word comes from
the vine, from an inventory of thirteen major
days: there lies a great puce-colored boulder.
Let me put you in the picture while blowing the
single-note half-hour call provoked by falsetto
screams, let me sell you the solid gold buddha.

2.

Front to front in an hour we stood, that face,
the Kremlin courtier, Kildare's sense of justice,
horizontal like the fronds of a fern: before a
hat-check congregation and its echoing retreat,
before the seating of grace on his brow, the
marks of a fool, horses turning to the right.
There is a damned book come here from beyond
the sea, there are spectacles on a body of
horsemen, cheerfully going towards death.
You will be astonished at the logic of ancestral
merchandise, the birdcage walk named after
the aviary denied the master. Nine children
died from want of mighty fabric, or breast
milk, leaf-producing points of solitude and
fatigue. Was there ever a mixed constitution
dominated by the middle part of the face?
Between the eyes, the waiters in uniform,
groves of lemon and orange, mingling notes
softened from below—as from God himself.

War

I am your naked Japanese proxying for health.
The moon blooms in occupied hours, printing
thumbnails of illiteracy on very good days.

A row of post-habilitated madams gossips
with the proctor in charge: affiliated lions
have escaped the zoo, hurtling through space.

At higher elevations, dolls have difficulty
breathing. I once noted on a rocky mountain
the sheltered lake running out of pure blue.

Everything is news, everything is distant
like one's own death, everything rejuvenates
silent old cells, puppets are turning into men.

At the auction house, tall labial figurines
of dust, women in Afro hats and Sardinian
smiles, pick the dried pockets of politicians.

Desex the flower of youth, whose patronage
in the trenches, amidst rotting legs and arms,
has led to centurion longevity for talking poets.

I've been holed up in this Roman villa,
mishearing the dirt hounds of afternoon,
for what seems to blurry visitors only a day.

the progress of sexuality

1.

sentence of walruses prolific sunbathing
barks groans hentai moans
labrador crocks furry and knowing
proprietary feet

2.

made me question
the chancellor of habits

3.

morning in sidereal Vietnam
burnt my intestines on coal
taped the broken backs of rickshaws
colored hermits' napes

4.

the hostile breast
under a single bulb
smiling open sky

5.

for lack of options

6.

my sister outfitted in rubber
plantation ruckus safety waddle
dynamite the ballplayer
who wore out his welcome
the smiling fiduciary aunts

7.

seedbed afternoons
how they decimate the fingering atrocities
little deaths o's and other vowels

8.

o climate of opinion
conditional genius bred on Kant's bed
miscellaneous investment opportunities
Kuwait Jhullunder Penang
women in betelnut red
lisping barefoot on clouds

9.

circular possibilities arrive as foiled haikus
the men of advertising are not mad
have the situationists ever won anything

10.

on the day they killed
fence behind which dragoons
fenders I warn skiers in blue
naked sullen tits grieve yellow
birth is forensic
minions to rhetoric

11.

block by block Antonioni culled
cycles of lunar puberty
the women of Capri sang
why not love Nabokov he

12.

shifted screens to Alexandria and the battle
went on at twice revolutionary speed Napoleon

13.

mingle air-conditioned air in the swamp sweat
the life of the balcony rose June
a summer's mise-en-scène dancers pickpockets chefs

14.

still it's not possible to find the backdoor
who broke open the alley
there are midgets conquering cornmeal police on ice

15.

here is a hacienda
in the volcano's eye
a stitch like Pinocchio's burns

16.

every ludic undergraduate
suffocates the yellow tit
the moon buried in New Orleans
witches the milk of human trust
wasted she rode me high higher than

17.

hitchhiked face like sunken moon on Route 9
past Ashbery's singing neutrality
China's trucks run aground and penguins' fracas
nobody's feces

18.

swollen

19.

a history of a Faulkner who went out of print
drank himself to death and 1952 rolled around
for festoons around nobility's arduous poles

20.

anorexic housewife
watching Aston Martins park
shoulder to shoulder

21.

lambsteak and humans
as the Japanese say levity
on the island of tomorrow evolution
of the game show for nephrous
time and inclination

confessions

i needed to arrive somewhere and the sooner the better
i would sit at my books until dinner-time with some philosophy book

logic of port-royal locke's essay malebranche leibniz or descartes
these polemics kept me very busy the first to fall victim

9 i was truly transformed 6 this fresh beginning led me by a new route
montesquieu broke off his friendship with father de tournemie

meaning nothing to the rest of the world i promise to forget your person
the same trust in charlatans that caused the grandson to perish

while at maman's i had completely lost my fondness for pilfering
through vigilance care and unbelievable effort nothing outside of ourselves

i became calmer and lost my enthusiasm for long journeys
our long habit of living and of living innocently together permitted

to a son though intoxicated too much to covet her clear in my own mind
was i happy not really i tasted pleasure her kind heart

i was an ardent frenchman and thus avid for news i had left
this kingdom i mocked the french over their defeats our little garden

lay at the top my soul in defiance of fortune has found to be truly good
the question arose as to where I was to stay i hardly dared breathe

flashed with the fire that burned in my veins ciceronian style untutored
locutions a passage behind her house to enter this door

she pitied me in my folly she wished to cure me of it i spared myself
i wish i could go on for ever talking about my candor shyness

mongmillon's machinations and his letters written from the mountain
silence in geneva all i had to do was enlarge at the height

of this frenzy of prosecutions and persecutions pierre boy was so stupid
i have told the truth i devised a strategy the alps dragging with me my age

The Man with the Movie Camera

At the end, roadside stilts, peasants
waltzing amongst their betters, burnt pink,
negating the crows of sudden grief.
A poolside miracle, the burly wrestler and his
Ellis Island bride, mating to muzak
played as thunder. Joy in pulling teeth,
opening up magical grocery stores,
sweeping stairs, paraphernalia of rust
and probability, each machine a mode
of tender value. If the birds die…
no, this is ever a distraction from the playful hunt.
I wash the ink off my thumbs in a washroom,
afraid the cornerless skyscrapers
have assumed Bauhaus manners while I
wasn't looking. Come and see
the grave my brother and I dug last night,
obeying the purges of our childhood.
Come and see the thin mountain air
animating bicycling girls, who laugh
as if no imitators had been born.

Cat

We are building a rainy boardwalk
on pretty legs of silence.
A man like bees looks under the tarp
and finds a row of sleeping gulls,
like paintbrushes in disuse.
A cloud spells our name in blue,
in the distance a funnel of water sprays
wobbliness on dozing children.
Home is a box of glue and sticks
spackled to our backs.

Without Which He Would Not Have Written His Greatest Poems

Use a lot of saliva to lubricate the lower part of the shaft, which you can stimulate with your hands. About Nietzsche, I am sorry to say that your suggestion had completely slipped from my mind. Do not zone in right away on the clitoris, and then rub away madly. The unphilosophical historian doesn't stay high on his ladder. The angle of her pelvis will enable the erect penis inside her to put sustained pressure on the front wall of the vagina and G-spot. Apparently the *Neue Rundschau* has not heard from him either. The man can thrust upward at the same time, but it may take a while to get the timing right together. About the Dutch literature. The man or woman can end up in a position in which the head is completely off the mattress and is resting against the floor. One might approve of the maintenance of The Church of England in our time and yet deplore its origin. Using your third and fourth finger, caress your clitoris and the surrounding areas in a cross-like movement, moving from north to south and then east to west, with your clitoris as the central point. By the way, I wrote some little time ago to Ortega y Gasset to ask him for a contribution and have had no reply. The man kneels back on his heels on the bed with the woman kneeling on top with her knees on either side of his. Having advanced so far, a Word of caution. Grip the top of the head like a water tap and twist as you would if turning a tap on or off. My policy is frankly a waiting one. You can roll your stockings down your legs—one at a time—either by yourself, or involve your partner in the action. I agree with you about Christ and I do not disagree with anything else. If being tied to the bedpost while your partner makes slow, tantalizing love to you or gives you orgasmic oral sex interests you and you plan to act it out, then make sure he or she does not tie the knots too tight, and that they can be undone immediately if you request it, or whenever necessary. On page 79 line 308 there are two commas to be deleted and I intended the four "burnings" to be printed with double spacing between each. The woman sits and raises one foot to point vertically over her head, steadying it with her hand. I am returning to you the "Metaphysical Posters" after long consideration. Purse your lips and then plant a light kiss, a little like a peck, but at the rate of about three a second. Oh I suppose the only thing to be done about W. Civilization is to think as clearly as one can. An armchair lends itself very well to rear-entry lovemaking, if the furniture is deep enough to take both partners on its seat. The style of wrappers is somewhat different here from that usual in America; they do not put on so much letterpress. There is no rule that dictates how often a couple should make love. I will buy a Cake.

IV.

Poets

i don't mean to presume uh every boy needs
poets in dream oboeland, oh my syrian robes
catch the first still summer-dew or late rain like
anxious amulets worn around wrung parrot necks
violets by mossy stones but she is in her grave
and softer than Galesian wool or phoenix rare
so send us topiaries of talking onyx centaurs
stableboys, horses smoldering before silence
glowing in the slow ashen crawl of spirits

Ars Poetica

We are stalling for time over the Grand Canyon's north rim,
as shadows of the century of no-war descend like hollow chalk,

putting our Rastafarian hearts in the shade, muting our twin
reindeer opposition: queer anonymous sleepers reappear,

Rip Van Winkle-like, as marooned camera eyes, layered in lost
yew off sunk deserts, repeating horoscopes for blind Everymans

hanging off ceiling-high bookshelves, finding passage to your seed.
Every rivulet here has had a name foretold for its peculiar destiny.

We dig up potato fields, maize, yarrow, whatever grows in the mirror
of the fallen yeti sky: famine disarrays free verse from its

stronghold on the linearities of colonial barter, man for man,
woman for woman, genitals pictured as nonce words, thick

sheaves of questions making scarecrows levitate to the rough winds.
There is no passion for missionary thirst. The blond beggars settle

quietly to refereed deaths in dark alleys overlooked by informants,
their children having long proceeded to islands buckled by paint.

I want to draw pictures of you. Without the sun chafing the leaves.

E.M. Forster in Alexandria

1.

The ghost ship, others did not look that interesting

2.

I shall be late over those geese or ducks
Wrong police court, did I send you the cinema one?
People walking across the hall at the Regina hotel

3.

This was not, of course, the majestic Ilium of Homer, but rather a seedy little tourist trap of a Troy that had grown up

4.

Crafty-ebbing accounts of the doings of the homosexual Maharajah
Who with, gently and just above the buttocks
Until my death and England's

5.

I understand you studied the Egyptian language. I congratulate you and myself, because now you will go to the city of Alexandria and teach boys at the teaching clinic of clyster[enema]-specialists of Phalu, and you will have provision for your old age.

6.

If I was rich I should build first an eye hospital then a Mosque
You can get friends if you have money except one or two
I wish I could talk Arabic to read the *1001 Nights*

7.

Defenders of the serapeum
The eye that is buried within us
Marble colonnades of the Street of the Soma

8.

I can't face the ethics of the thing
Preservation is my cry, I worship Vishnu
Digression: Do you know The Will as Vision?

9.

Chatby, Sporting, Ibrahimiya, Cleopatra, Stanley, Glymenopoulo, San Stefano, Sidi
Bishr, Miami, Asafra, Mandara, Montaazah, Maamoura

10.

He sang (Iago's credo) and very splendidly he sang
I wish you could have seen them asleep on the decks at night
Oh I feel so obscure, the breast of my British Red Cross tunic

11.

One Sunday morning they visited Pompey's Pillar and the Kom el Shogafa
catacombs, on another they went out to the Nouzha Gardens, or sometimes of an
evening they would return to the ducks at the Municipal Gardens in the middle of
town.

12.

The sanctuary of the oracle alone

13.

Scene Heaven a staircase stretching indefinitely
Aged footsteps far below
No persons will loiter within the vicinity of these steps

14.

Listen to the notes, to the exquisite instruments of the mystic choir,
and bid farewell to her, to Alexandria whom you are losing

15.

Going either from his flat to the office, or from his office to his flat

16.

A minor post in the Department of Irrigation
The larger Arabian salon with its Oriental-looking furniture
Sometimes the traffic murders it, a petrol lamp if night had fallen

17.

I leave Egypt in comparative content
A real Missionary magazine, Shazad is gratifying
I am lying in bed waiting for my breakfast

18.

My native town, oh my native town!
The military authorities have taken my boy.

19.

The motor car and the bus and the great extension of the bathing habit

20.

What if he could sail west to Cathay?
What if the book he held in his hands that day was correct?
A book from the library at Alexandria.

21.

At the house of Mohammed's friend the matrimonial agent, or on a hillside near Mex, where they sat "as Maurice and Clive sat at Cambridge."
Where would I be if I had gone for "requiring" things like Plugs and Plates?
Why do you not take them costlier gifts? Why not take them a pair of Egyptians?

22.

I hate a boy whom any man can have, nor do I drink from a public fountain.

23.

He was only thirty-one. Novelists today mature more slowly.
But don't ever marry Agnes, as though that were likely.

24.

I leave here poorer by a kiss.
"Like a king," Porus said simply.
The phalanx moved on.

25.

The obverse of love is not hatred but fear.
To merge myself. To test myself. To do my bit.
Damn justice, damn honor.

26.

When you are in love with one of its inhabitants, a city can become a world.

27.

Or with olives, their possibilities and price, or with the fortunes of friends, or George Eliot, or the dialects of Asia Minor.
You could never understand my poetry, my dear Forster, never.
Pray that you, you English with your capacity for adventure, never lose your capital, otherwise you will resemble us, restless, shifty, liars.

28.

Amr's horsemen rode through the Gate of the Sun
4,000 palaces, 4,000 baths, 400 theatres, 1,200 greengrocers, 40,000 Jews
They destroyed her, as a child might a watch

29.

Mud-moving, a feebler India
Semi-East or pseudo-East
Mud, the mud of the Nile

30.

Oh, you are quite sufficient, sir, let us keep a lady out of it, no need to drag in a lady.
Heaven bless the ladies! I have just wasted the whole morning over those geese or ducks.
Now you can buy an English book. The sum is too small for a book.

31.

The Syrians dance.
The Bedouins lay eggs.
The French give lectures on Kultur to the French.
The English have witnessed "Candida" or "Vice Detected."

32.

That's a Mosque for _____ (I beg your pardon) M.'s.
One of my greatest friends (i.e. Masood) was a Moham[?].
I want to ask you a question about Mohammedans, which please answer truly, sir.

33.

O my dear the sanitation!
How will it end?
"Morgan I will hurt you," "Edward I will kill you"—until they fell asleep.

34.

Shymaking and threnodic,
during the heyday of cosmopolitan Alexandria,
the unlikely figure of a Philadelphia judge.

The Beats

on the advice of Paul Bowles, in 1950 he moved to Tangier
with that little camera that he raises and snaps with one hand
on a gray day, abandoned tin cans and old building blocks

his wild eye, a "real" American, sucked such a poem right
out of America, with that little camera he raises and snaps with
one hand, the crazy feeling in America, the result is America

get an old panel truck for $95 and be your own Monastery in it,
Walden Pond a Disneyland outpost, one hand, the crazy feeling in
America, Buddhism was psychic junk, unspoken despair

who informed Allen that "gold is the measure of genius," weeping
and undressing while the sirens of Los Alamos wailed them down,
be your own Monastery in it, conducted by actors and their friends

"put down your cigarette rag," gold is the measure of genius,
a ninety-year-old butoh dancer at the Japan Society, rigor mortis,
salvation by singing, which is why he was our Whitman, rhapsodic

on the bells of the old Dutch church in the center of the circular town,
a ninety-year-old butoh dancer at the Japan Society, fetus in a bottle,
Ike's rounded face, secret committees, bald head and blank stare

the car featured thirteen upside-down American flag decals
oversimplifying the poet's vision, fetus in a bottle, Ike's rounded
face, we see God through our assholes in the flash bulb of orgasm

asking Joan to balance a glass on her head in Mexico City in the fall
of 1951, through our assholes, seized by a recurrent ugly spirit,
six fabulous places in the Gobi Desert one hundred thousand years ago

a ticket for decay, American jeeps, the Gobi Desert one hundred
thousand years ago, Peace-Eye Bookstore, an Ankah symbol tattooed
on his penis, blood vessels on the mimeograph exploded in Tangier

Enemies in Bed

More and more it seems to me that this Jeffersonian phrase is what we think about when we think about the American dream.

Prairies outside dormant cities, America of dreams!
When the Egyptian confidence room opened, she looked pretty
She had him eating nasturtiums out of a symbolic tube
Of yesterday's restored brush-stroke emblems.
I'm from Cincinnati which is to this place's nominative like a remote dative
Sky woof woof! harp is published in *Semicolon*
I think poems are esthetecologically harmless and psychodegradable
Writing constantly, in any case, is the poetic dream

The adventures of art and education were a reward for having fought the good war.

Now it has happened yesterday
The long dusty path there
A long line of lyricists
Starting with Lope
The engine is gentle, a lakeside hotel
And I made an amazing zinc airliner
Cherrywood avalanche, my statue of you
Near a blaze of straw

Has there ever before been such an assortment of people who have found such an assortment of things to set their teeth on edge?

Summer in the trees!
To be roughed up by the trees
To the sound of canoes
I misunderstand Renaissance life
Ancient China, the Middle Atlantic States
All of whom I love!
The Russian poet appears
Creamy female marble.

The dialect of the tribe was meant to be not purified but perpetuated, warts and all, without apology or attack.

In opera librettos, or even in one's life
Different civilizations, simultaneously existing
One being peaceful or horrid or lonely or bored
Five flights up the June street, eighty-five days
As beautiful as an orchestra or a cup
My life, and only one life, one death
Later thousands of dreams, I read

The streets and bars were full of writers and painters and the kind of young men and women who liked to be around them.

In summer the abstract words
Where Sunday mornings spell
She is also your daughter
And staying on the boat
Often ready to be inquired
Testimony to live valentine
The sum is divine and you are out
Accordions I couldn't be sure

Among the educated classes, Freudian psychoanalysis achieved a sudden popularity that gave rise to the suspicion that neurosis was the universal human condition.

He was sorry to be so nervous
No soft breast, no soft bottom
Beside the white un-analyzed chickens
No École des beaux arts in this part of town
But there's nothing like American foam
But I am suffering all the same
Oh we are still together sometimes
To be alive at all is to amaze someone
Or trees with a breeze for a mouth

Internet Celebrity

After Michael McClure

Value-added language
freighted with machinery
of silent birds caught in the rumors of war:

hand-looms and weaves, factories of quiet
TOLSTOY-MADE ENDLESS
DECADES OF "WHAT LITERATURE IS ALL ABOUT"
IN THE MIDDLE BRAINS
OF THE CRITICS

who have fanned and faved me
for knowing two ounces more than themselves.

THE DEATH OF THE AUTHOR,
THE DEATH OF THE NUCLEAR BOMB,
THE DEATH OF THE POSEIDON ADVENTURE

and I wait hallucinating under my mushroom roof
looking for water
in all the tidy sexes,

looking for whole bread
in the talking bin of cash.

Saying
FUCK YOU
TO STRANGERS
WHO WOULD NEVER MOLEST YOUR CHILD
is sometimes acceptable

if you do it breaking out of mountains
of male modesty,

and the children don't have to be bribed
to applaud.

If you do it
in a nether web of awareness,
the plain meaning of sex,
the common language of family,
the frank protocol of meals.

AT HOME
scampering bicycles
stand nodding their blue lamps by the open garage door,
flickers of polite recognition
passing between neighbors.

It's all right to say
fuck you
TO STRANGERS
if you have launched them
on the tumorous questioning
following a full stomach
and an empty night's rest.

Otherwise, cut the silly
adverbs please,
cut them out of the frigid essay,
take their shape and invent a new head for yourself,

recumbent, Greek/classic, high-profiled,
visible in the mucky atrophies of the OED,
so far from the origins of hate you're afraid
like horses in war,

horse-shapes in the war,
convoluted O-mouths,
war-cyclicals, Pentagon papers, leaks and verbiage,
so many mouths in need of a hard slap,

a little blood,
a few drops of suffering,

and
NONSENSICAL
JAZZ RIFFS ISSUING FROM HOUSEWIVES'
CORNERED BRAINS

as if TV was everywhere.

Oscar Wilde

Charlotte Charlotte Charlotte
slight violet-eyed if never very good
whistler I like this I don't like that

being a gentleman fifty years earlier
Queen of Romania Princess Christian Marie Corelli
write one line of poetry serious or comic

one of many graceful figures
destructive and self-destructive elements
the most infamous brute in London

they laugh angrily at his epigrams
you have no appreciation for literature
if you had asked me for fifty

brilliant pastiche portrait
phallic bouquet of carrots and turnips
he was turned away, posing Sodomite

await the poet's return
incriminating evidence, common gossip
heads of the five hundred noblemen

erotomane who loved nothing more
looking shabby, worn and threadbare
and outcasts always mourn

Mountolive

our egypt our beloved country
extempore such as one has sometimes heard
a tremendous silence
desert preachers before they fall into a trance
broke through the veil
candle-light like a musical instrument
the silence which follows some great performance
the germinal silence
fecundated
and so on
the nile, the green river, offspring of st. mark
that voice! stiff as a javelin
a terrified curate in a badly-ironed surplice
spontaneous flights of drunkards
billiard singers, burial processions, death-diving poetry
softly about like honey
flood of rhetoric, knotted again
then came a change
sprawling, like music, descendants of the pharaohs
abrupt as a metal shutter coming down
a silence impossible to repair again
almost impatiently
an electric current had begun to pour
his muscles, his loins
smiling like a dog, that voice
words like chain-shot
impossible to paraphrase the matter
a sort of wooden lectern with a candle burning
taking place behind the white walls

The Habit of Novel Reading

Patriotic citizens cast an evil eye on you,
Christ is your life and rent, inscription in a
house that nature lends such evil dreams:
he was the worst geometrician of all mortal
men, printed all his book, the chapel door
the force of a rule, ordered the kings copies
of laws. His Master's presence will reward.
Archetypal diminutive monstrous farrow,
the light stroke of a hammer, these I call
farraginous, in the distance a pure cottage,
preserved to admiration of gypsy qualities.
Then out came from a fictionary uncle's
care the father of that child, legal fiction,
too formless to inspire the food of song.
He examines the fid-hook and the dog-
hook, which the king could not take but
the knight could, collecting cards and all
the petty fiddlefaddle that is growing stale.
The plank is said to fay to the timbers,
famine, war, and effete races to be reckoned,
farthingale chairs designed for ladies in
wide skirts. He works in metal, stone, wood,
the fabric and constitution of our mind in
which an angular notch has been cut out.
Transmutation of mother rock, resembling
flagella, a single row of tentacles, not only
fumes but visible steams: these new wants
attract an ever-growing army of recruits.
Will you give up eternal columns in the
broadsheet? The errata put immediately
before the body of work, a cocked hat of
equilateral dimensions, extinct ungulates.

V.

Autobiography of a Graffiti Villain

1.

I capsize newspapers in water. I shake myself free of watchwords. I hang balloons on wounded sticks, the balcony gold-latticed on the truant morning, the moon a waxy after-effect smudged like conversation. Music, lavish and omnipresent, squeezes between drachmas and bangles. My deck of cards falls like a waterfall. My mother calls me inside in a voice splintered like a thousand bees on the same mission. Sunlight washes over my soft thighs and knees like a baby's croons. The fly's intermittent buzz reminds me of forgotten lessons. Time is a century of turquoise pools facilitating suicide. My first watch is a gift of anxiety. Now seconds count. How long can I hold my breath? Palm trees whip in the wind like runaway children. My mother calls again, from the other side of the moat, unable to tickle my ears. A line of ants, curving like serious S's, forecasts future earthquake cracks. The dark stairways of my hundred-year-old building steal me like a pasha's only son, hunting in the garden alone at night, kissed by talented witches. The weight of the building is like ten earthquakes occurring simultaneously in a moment. Yellow and red almirahs unfurl their metal skin for a stolen touch or two, laughing at their open secrets. Each morning is like every other until I split it open, the street is a parade ground for costumed vendors with voices like melons, the smell of boiled potatoes makes me believe no one can ever be sick or poor. I steal time and the world lets me. My mother calls a last time, fanning herself with the lazy newspaper. I ought to be a child detective like in my favorite books, but the tar streets and black palms and drunk pools are too friendly, they all want to pat me, they won't fight back.

2.

A woman too old to be in college has whispered in these rooms like a rented ghost. Saffron threads erase the schooled boxes of thoughtlessness on the ochre walls. The rooms get tinier the more we inspect their need to doze. On the balcony my sister and I observe a row of naked workers languidly masturbating on the street. I want to start a company that makes designer jeans for women only. My eye has an erasable splinter, making me see double only in the mornings. I attach "Kick me" signs on the backs of professional activists when I'm not mocking the death of God. My dreams swirl inside the small dark closet along with Malcolm X's bitumen gaze and hands like guns. Please keep my secret, pleads the girl next to me in class, whose face will one day grace magazines for secretaries. I'm poor like the mice buried under the marble floor. My mother and father discuss the price of the house and echoes bounce off walls, like religions fading out. My sister points to a livid star in the afternoon sky, a cosmic joke she ought to share with the blooming wisteria overhanging the iron gate. College students across the street carry crates of flags, smuggling them into the classroom for a revolution of the medieval mind. Years later I will hear of polite ways of torture that can be denied. This neighborhood of the legitimate rich is soaked in the paranoia of genitals attached to brainless wires. I want only a small room crammed to the ceiling with masks and funnels. On the street my sister and I spot a bawdy van, scrawled on which are the names and numbers of the most hated politicians. I wish I possessed the megaphone that will usher in the last day, mountains crumbling like fluffy cotton. My feet are joined to the rosy marble, I am a pink statue foolish enough to bask in the sun, my last thought is to strangle my well-wishers.

3.

The island abounds in secretaries saturated with the odor of their bosses' reedy madness. Rats conduct operatic orgies on sentinel coal, their napalm saliva dragged across the dark remains like man forced on the moon. My pockets fall open, tramps declared lost in the newspapers spill out, a whore or two in Saturday finery, priests sodomized by God. Gay men are getting rough-voiced just around this time, also getting hold of guns. The island has pockets of inspired poverty known as villages, where sculptors of the neutral universe insist theirs is a world apart. I do not want to be Oliver Twist to their Fagin. Once in the gold-stalactite lobby of the second tallest building on earth I find, in a damp newspaper, an ad for an escort who gets along well with monkeys and cobras. I make myself invisible in a phone booth, crawl up a sea-bred lady's stockinged legs, my soul the similitude of a buttercup. Her companion comes to her rescue, a golden man in a tireless suit, hair slicked back, the smell of child love on his breath. This is what they want to make of me, a child or an animal, a high-strung new woman dressed in young boy's clothes. I like to walk the length and breadth of the island, fighting off window reflections, a guerilla afraid of sniper fire. My spine lengthens during these excursions, my head swells until I bandage it with the derelict past. In certain circles populated by the old rich, eddies whirl around, pulling into their orbit all the little men and women in love with their own television voices. Once I try to save a girl from being swallowed with the rest, and she smacks my face, telling me she comes from the tropics, don't I know what that means? Off-duty policemen scrutinize my fellating walk. These are the days the people of the island decide bankruptcy is not an option. There has not been a real war in a decade, panic is setting in. I try to remember home in my own voice but it comes out as Buddhist chants. Ordinary commuters take leave of ordinary families, domiciled in the paperback demonic, so many it's like the ocean switching currents.

Bookseller

Foolish darkness, have you not heard Stephen Hawkings's natural voice? My mind is a Piccadilly muddle, surprised at the wrong turns, nullified by the pubs and their mobbing patrons. The centuries totter on top of each other, unable to rest. In Florence they took me for a predator, though the boys for once were friendly with the pope. A young girl read me a haiku and it was as if I were a bee trapped in a flower, my death an imminent sun. In this moldy shop, cubism is a disorder we value, it comes with the rewards of childlessness. Some say cows have minds, some say monkeys have souls, some say snails understand time. I found myself unable to come for years at a time. Then when the party of ribald sailors visited me, on the darkest Friday of the winter, they promised mountains of snow, and it was like the earth settling to a new equilibrium. There was a cinema across the street where they showed grainy Buñuel, and I met many a tireless woman there. I would have been a nobody in the Crusades, not even a cheering bystander. Fallow those apples of the Eve-bungled paradise, where my Satan would have fellated the couple, everyone's hands tied behind their backs. Alice in Wonderland holes, canyons projecting with the eye of a needle and mines covered over with chalk, so watch your step. Since the first shipwrecked sailor, islands have been caricatured, like women too faithful to one man. I mind my own business, sweep the dust off periodicals and newspapers with arms mechanized by medieval talents. The Buddhists say empty your mind, and I say my habitat is that emptiness. Poof, and like a fountain of dust all the souls that art curated soundlessly fall on a bookmark the size of my thumb. There are trapdoors leading to libraries from other universes, where illustrations are transferred from the mind to the page with the power of will, so watch where you grope. My first wife is buried somewhere here. I thought today was Sunday, or perhaps Tuesday, but relativity has seized me in my ancient boots: What is the day and time and year, name it, you fool!

Objects

1. Kettle

Chiffon love, rumor from a railroad, holding your nose at breath of waters: fey lovelies have endangered salmon-centuries to habitate short canyons of delight. Fuel stifles Mediterranean longevity, whistling for Seferis's eyesight. I am a fire-closed chaparral in a Sunday altercation. Laughter in a pancreatic doze, a hot affair at the farm, windows closed. O steam, O calculus of middle age, O minor steel goddess, give us rest.

2. Wall

A swollen Che hand, bursting through the other side of history, like dead fish or obedient commanders or Hemingway prose. Volcanoes are passé. Nude beauties squat like primitives, tired of the abuse in the family van. At the last moment the officers change their mind and condemn the poet to instant death. Love, sputtering like a car out of fuel, made over into teal workshops and stanzaic collapse.

3. Mat

A different piazza every morning, to sell my immaculate body, but the same customers. The elegance with which Françoise Sagan said no to lusting publishers. Only translate! How corny the fees imposed on late-returned books, as though books had feelings. Some women have all the luck, born into privilege, fetish of panthers. I stand still in a world of beauty, rising from the clumps of the earth, like a hard-earned promotion.

4. Jacket

Priests who outlive Irish intransigence, murmur into the swallowing mouths of canonical texts. I find Derrida comical. On the road to bestiality, many a minor corruption, strengthening the irredentist soul. A deliriously ill bird comes to my window and I act as though it is myth incarnate. Rape and dark don't go together. I raise my right hand, swearing the truth, and notice the death-defying glimmer in the judge's eyes.

5. Apple

Design is a problem for undergraduates. The elegant bushwhacking versus the array of bulldozers. Often I fall ill from contentment. I know how it is inside remote monasteries, where love is memorized in discriminating couplets. No one taught me fear. I know all the circles of hell, which is the most abstract conception of all, its eggshell definition slender as the membrane between truth and lies. I invented freedom.

Matisse, *The Moroccans* (1916)

A pause on a black Friday in the barter of souls, and the posture of whatever smiles on behalf of hashish. A mad morning stone-decked like the blustery walls of prayer. A virgin in search of thirst. Minus solemn chants, minus refusal of brides, minus the wickedness of acquired languages. The dictionary open like the ladder to anonymity. Effaced, nourished like a newborn, the round music of the not-desert. Nothing connects like habituality. Day-glow for a foreign master, a limit to robed capitulation, a folded crouch toward the black core of terrifying discourse.

VI.

Letters to Y.

1.

Whose arms like pentangles of scenery shared
in silkworm eclipses, peonies bringing me edu-

cated guesses about Edwardian electricity and
its ecumenical deck chairs; whose clematis a

carved calendar, meaning a horoscope of hope,
pipes marinated in silent marching orders you

and I hear as medicine, nestled in intervening
octaves. Pink is the color, a warm ecology of

layers of effacement, rood screen behind which
our rooms of snow-white treaties are zipped,

like bags on furlough, then unzipped in a fuzz
making your skin and its dewberry bloom detect-

able. Pink is the color, warm echo of form so
delicately brachial it needs a new name to speak.

My hospitality is Nazarene when it's not near-
sighted, that is to say, it is a tiny percussion cap

whose per diem fits your scheme, it is terra
firma, it is a galliard we will dance like colts.

2.

The sixteenth note of beauty, a vexatious
safflower vibrato, to which we trace our

interviews of the morning of the goldfish
bowl: please let me hide the old behind your

golden neck and decipher the age of courage.
We left dusty caryatids in the casbah of chains

behind, and mingled with the mimics milling
around humidly, humoring our hurricane

lamps. What comes of beauty as it erodes
night after night the escapades of our noms

de plume? Would you call me a nonperson
because I have ideas about igloos wherein

you fit like an illusion? Watch how the
margay strides the fallen branches, like

objets d'art come to life in the most obvious
scamper. Does your scansion show my

umbilical cord attached to peaceable umiaks
traveling along a moving sea of fossils?

3.

The easel at the end of the world besides
which sequesters your forties hat and your

sonatina smile as near as the field glasses
we made friends with: lunette aperture,

moon-lit, mood of nexus, nimbus around
ovules of winter. The rule is to generate

gold leaves at the fine epicenter and stand
back to watch the ever-diminishing crown,

like cosmonauts making cameos to break
through carrels of glass. In that hat and

that smile duende is subject to due process,
finches fill the gestalt of incidental music,

lacquer metabolizes the séanced music box,
sunbursts summersault for our sympathy,

and the fiasco of the fez is forgotten. You
burst through the diorama of the cosmos

in a camisole of nimble second guesses,
festal lifeline to petals of dry powder.

4.

The wild card was that you were in a province
of sweet fennel, wilting but not wilting, limping

but not limping, custodian of square pegs. You
are rustic in my rustic home, contrapuntal when

it counts most, converging toward the carina of
the carriage house. Part song, partitioned slip

knot, theater-in-the-round weary of the theorems
of dictionary usage: do we still believe in capri

pants, do we know cantalinas slim as the breath,
do we average out the red shift when calculating

the schoolgirl's seven days of tongue-twisting?
The finest vellum is in that drawer to your right,

where you can write me as flautist to liqueurs,
link to the stylus which scratches woven homes.

You cannot be weary except in multiples of
forty, the fortune teller in you snowballing to

the vibrations of houndstooth epitaphs: we two
wrote the equipoise dangling like a cowbell.

5.

Metonymy functions in the northern lights,
scarlet and schismatic, as the slow thresh of

Cinderella, the ciliary body of bohemian or
cicada pathfinders, somebody's solution to

solitary confinement. Pensive, are you solo
constituency in the cellar of awakenness, or

is your apocrypha sundered in the sunshade?
This winter will be the best ever, I promise.

Do you want more brainteasers? Shall I go
on with the brass band, or license the clavier

to perform nothing and then nothing else
like a pastoral in tailspin? Follow me to the

taiga and you will remain colorfast, pastel
book asserting its pigeonhole, combustible,

yes, but always the piccolo I dreamed as
your physique: resource of sunblock, drunk

eardrum dwelling like a cowl on pentecost
falling like trivia on the stewards of rain.

6.

Vanilla matadors, electable matchbooks,
edelweiss from next-door Eden on a pretty

waterbed (though I never saw your bed-
room), waves of masterkeys to farmlands

we see in no way castellated: will you have
me over again? I could catapult past your

buffet, or the buffer zone, and get into shape
like a shareholder, or shareware, and we

could sip café du monde in water repellant
flattery—except I mean to say not flattery

but the dimmer we turn on, ignoring Hazel
Basil, our private cassette of Carthusian sub-

culture, meditations on viburnum's air of
phlogiston, the last of the philosophical

phobias, and prying open the phylacteries
of minor coliseums: it is all there in bi-

nomial poverty, self-chosen, that is to say,
terrace to the vanishing point of white light.

7.

Altar to whole tone scale (nova!), like life
insurance in a cold whorl of chocolate, or

those home movies shown at ferris wheel
festivals, fictive duties all: what is your

time frame, or is that even a question?
Once upon a time I used to be a futurist.

Until further notice, epoxy will arrive
episodically, and still lifes shall command

a tenth of their usual price. When you
read these poems to me I think of Venn

diagrams of verismo (think Puccini),
and plan to deflate all the remaining

versicles occupying the deferential
clutter. I would be content with a bunk-

house, the burr we hear in mineral
water, the summer solstice if and when

it comes. This wadi was hollowed out
from within its witnesses to honeydew.

8.

It is not for me to be demonstrative.
The rituals carrying us past the riptide

stymie all but the stuttertone we hear
in top-heavy eyelashes. I follow de-

corum to the decimal point. Maltese
cross borne by the sika is like silent

commerce, telling me the way to your
silky signature. Is a troika better?

I would describe your energy as la-
crosse among the medaka, fleur-de-lis

responding to the stooping of stone
masons, cytology for doodlebug czars.

Mine, as you know, is doomsday at
the doorbell, dolman sleeve for every-

one else's take-home pay, wainscot
flooded last time and walking out like

a xylene yawn. But I have every hope
that the rosebud concerto will be wild.

9.

The kiss was a garland in the luster
around the Milky Way, the whisper

of the luna moth in the marshlands:
Old English shogun that I used to be

in the stillbirth of my ambition, I am
faithful now to figurines swallowing

the dauphin. A cloud of pine martens
rises from the burgundy leather couch

where you have shown me some of
your starlit works that are the opposite

of trachism, collages that are taber-
nacles of femininity, mitzvah mixed

up with mockingbird salaams. Kiss
me, kiss me again and again, scherzo

on French leave, kiss me so I can
feast on the farthest evangelism, kiss

me like a lullaby of the evening star,
kiss me till I am a torn rhododendron.

10.

When you explain your art to me, I think
of how expression is malleable, not in the

way the masking of maladies is, or spectacles
of madras madwomen, but magnifications,

growing out of first names and first person,
creating an epic environment not just as

decoy but to let the cutworm in at the back.
Yes, this house was surely a speakeasy

where they overstayed visas and ovulating
retirees modeled for terra cotta. But your

soft feet walking on these Javanese floors
make this house lighter than air, liliaceous

novena for December. Your art is nostalgia
observed in pearlescent hierarchies, heyday

of the ground squirrel, glass ceiling at rest
like iridium along the iris, gypsy moth I

have loved since I was firestone, exposing
marginalia taken from the schoolhouse.

11.

What can I say about your feet that
talismans can talk over? Your feet are

the topic of my uppercase upbringing,
washing over hagiographia of glare

ice. Thank you for painting your toe-
nails that bright red. It reminded me

of failing to educate myself in ducal
oversight. There is an optic nerve for

rituals of satori, known only by sun
fish. Do you know, princess of the

summerhouse (or my upstairs porch),
the temple of worship where they

make their entrance as ephemera?
Your feet are the epicycle whose

economies of diffidence I defer to.
I was imprisoned in the jardinière,

sleepy like sonar, but to touch you
is to come back to my first solitude.

VII.

Loneliness

Only boxers understand the loneliness
of tennis players, maybe we were meant to be
lonely, maybe we were meant to be on our own.

"What's a million dollars compared to the love of eight million Cubans?"

We were boxing, we were boxing the stars.
We were boxing, you were swinging from Mars
for the love of boxing. Together in its rawest state:
from fear to hatred, from euphoria to loneliness,
from heroism to sadness.

Nobody ever lies about being lonely.

To most people, the two-word pitch for Real Steel
—"boxing robots"—probably sounds a little silly.
And I love underdog movies—*Rocky* and *Hoosiers*.
Sugar Ray talked to me a lot
about the loneliness of the sport.
And, unfortunately, loneliness can be unhealthy
beds that wet themselves in the morning,
and an entirely new sensation called loneliness.

My arms…my arms are too short to box with god.

Aren't you supposed to be eternally in love with him and shit?
Oh, I thought I was gonna have to spend my dowry
on booze and pills to numb the loneliness.
Users become the living embodiment of loneliness
and gain the ability to become strong by being alone.

Loneliness is not something that strikes
the poor, unpopular, or unattractive.

Boxer Floyd Mayweather has OBSCENE amounts of money
in your Cheerios, this plea of LONELINESS may make you
THROW UP. Wow, you have it REAL BAD FLOYD!
I guess money CAN'T BUY you LOVE or FRIENDS!

We were boxing, you were swinging from Mars.

A wall inscription of one word is evident
behind the boxers and the audience:
The shots of Rocky's back suggest
his feelings of loneliness and hopelessness.

Loving the loneliness.
"Well, I think the veal died of loneliness."
Taught us nothing else, and it hasn't,
it's that girls should stick to girls' sports,
such as hot oil wrestling and foxy boxing and such and such.
I work hard, and I love my kids.

Then more T.V.
And maybe a lonely can of beer before bed.
"I mean, no matter how well it's going sexually or love-wise or both,
the day arrives when it's over."

Let me sit here with my loneliness, let me keep the shreds,
'cause they are the only give.

I agree animals do give unconditional love
through the bone-crunching, no-holds-barred
Japanese boxing industry. On the surface,
Tsukamoto's tale of love, loneliness, and loose teeth.

They love each other.
There is no loneliness like theirs.
At home once more, they begin munching
the young tufts of spring in the darkness.

I know the psychology of success and the loneliness.
I am in the executive search and team.

We all know that Valentine's Day means either
loneliness or love and jewelry,
it's the loneliness that's the killer, so you want,
heal with time, shoot that love, there is no other.

The cut in which sounds made by events
occurring in the image (the boxing gloves).

There is another kind of love that is not for beauty's sake.
Every day I am face to face with their loneliness
and their pride and their loves and their hunger.
I had just come from a hard workout,
part boxing, part meditation.

The source claims Monica has more or less
given up on finding love.
I feel foolish and I am very lonely most of the time.
I am paid very little.
All the time he's boxing, he's thinking it's
the One in Which Your Love for Each Other
Exceeds Your Need for Each Other.

The spy will always love them:
007's former sidekicks still know how to.
I love that Anne Morrow Lindbergh
chose the word "loneliness."

Loneliness is essentially independent.
They will find she was wearing boxing gloves.
If we played cultural Fantasy Boxing League,
and made books go 15 rounds.

Surveillance

Airman of superfluous moisture,
cried Leonard in Wednesday's
column: void of air, breezeless,
when the tender couples are up

at the eight-aired musical box.
A ferment which behaves like
contemplation: we may speak of
one and the same negligence.

Altering man's mood has abuse
capability, I dare not promise
abundance of breath, excursions
in number theory. The serpent

in me meets at a single point of
aberration, flavored with jack-
boots and parents turning away.
Veneered with avodire, dealing

ritually with anthropophagi, we
pass into the belly to be voided.
Art-worm, the day of interment
economizes space, the hypo-

thetical second earth dancing
on paper is an error in printing.

Mussolini

granted I am space under viaducts
open (cycling fencing skiing) helmet princes
dark princes their eyes fixed on distant
dark lands unoccupied by Romans
figure of eight spinning in a block of ice
I like your way of saluting on the piazza
hunkered down for the end of time
wheat girls, pinions in the marshes
balustrades that end in question marks

Controlled Demolition

My life was not mine anymore:
temperature, blood pressure, height, weight, heart rate, pulse, pending medication,
fetishism of organizational form,
the smashing of the state.
You can do this in America,
dress yourself in a drugstore from head to toe,
which I admire quietly.

Nothing surprises me.
If history were cyclical, we would now be in a decadence, would we not,
Heidegger against Heidegger,
why do I stay in the provinces,
an entity may even insist upon its figures solely to remain more present,
the way data dissolves at one end of the series just as it takes shape at the other,
reading an avant-garde western called *Existentialist Sheriff*.

Which street will we occupy?
Strange Christianity, the virtual is the invisible X,
the void whose contours can only be reconstructed from its effects,
now I'm on death row (the top lists of the surrealists):
three tiers of data running concurrently a hundred feet above the street,
first I stole the money, then I lost it.
No debts outstanding, either way.

If this makes me sexier, then where are you going?
A person rises on a word and falls on a syllable.
I'm changing the subject, I look at books and drink brandy.
So who are these workers who produce the city?
The word feral pulled me up short,
the feral media, nihilistic and feral teenagers, feral capitalism hits the streets,
our rapid-response team,
God is unconscious.

The Real Transported Man:
a son passes nothing back up.
Is old age a disease?
It's the strongest marriage in the world.
Violent overthrow is a Christian phenomenon.
Nobody's overloading the system or manipulating our sites.
Where do all these limos go at night?

You must set him among the dead.
Capital is automatically valorized by its own powers.
I'm susceptible to global strains of illness.
He was killed live on the Money Channel.
F-U-C-K-E-Y Y-O-U-S-E.
Considerate of them, grasp this moment,
fictional amounts of money, fictions built upon fictions.
In reality it is a summary court in perpetual session.

Translations from Lorca

1. Farewell

If I die the internet buzzes on.
A little boy shaving his cute moustache,
fingers of ice-cream,
trailing vapors of dissonance
behind the already-dead mother
laced in gunpowder.

2. Suicide

The girl and her paltry bathtub.
The stigmata of science fiction roses.
A garrulous morning outside the
hedonist balcony, facing the glass
tower of silence. How many
wires of torture run through this
gay workers' paradise?

3. Narcissus

You came to my banquet a flabby boy.
I jittered obese skin from zero to zero.
Boy, give me your death rays,
your video coronations, your stalactites
of corn and cocaine and cadence.
You speak like a Brooklyn sodomite.
A naked palm tree hallucinates
your next moment of death.

4. In Another Mode

We walk across the dynamite bridge.
The business school has a face of indigestion.
You wonder about the organs of my name.
I am on my death-spiel about bureaucrats.
Some think airports are paradises.
I touch your rose skin with my name,
before the mullahs rise for prayers.

5. Desire of a Statue

To be looked at on rainy afternoons
beside the halls of Iron Curtain greatness
like a redeemed possibility, bride
to gestures, twice the ordinariness
of supermarket shopping, hollow eyes
tracing the signifier settling down,
sighing, giving up torture,
compromising for food or drink.

Weight

city lights has reissued lew welch's selected poems
with an introduction by gary snyder who found the suicide
note at his northern california home though the body was never

recovered i'm sure this qualifies for commondreams as a new
poetry book with political charge yesterday i visited the indie bookfest
at menil under the awning shadowing art with my fingertips

like my fellow sunburnt hedons on our last hebraic legs the silence
of beckett muteness in the face of failure failing to surprise
is no less than a rodeo riding my chest stretched to lascivity

in the school of picaro these forty years feel like a glimpse
of an embryonic time-scale tarkovsky's pace a silent film stalled
on the first intertitle the one that tells you the hero embodies

virtuous character the births and rebirths of the novel
from the point of view of '82 says leslie fiedler is a worry
i can't stop fiddling about I declare the pop novel dead in

the arms of the art novel and both of them weightless
propositions the seminar of abstraction where the implied reader
sits in self-judgment ted berrigan died young too an old

man singing the praises of childlessness because no great
poet leaves an heir what is your greatest fear child of
spiders a bulk over my skull i cannot stultify yet

the nights darkening lips with baroque breath
not the flippant ecclesiastics i was promised

Alexandria in World War II

The Britannia Club at 26 Rue Fuad, "proof of the British ability":
we danced with Durrell's future friend the painter Clea Badaro
during the summer the Burg el Arab served as base for Indian troops,
the long-threatened concert party having descended in force.

We danced with Durrell's future friend the painter Clea Badaro,
marching about in a snake dance including the band at the Excelsior,
the long-threatened concert party having descended in force.
Since spring, Geneva has thrown open her home to soldiers.

Marching about in a snake dance including the band at the Excelsior,
air raid in the middle, buffet afterwards, breakfast for sixteen.
Since spring, Geneva has thrown open her home to soldiers,
the Choremis, the Benachis, the Casullis, the Salvagos and others.

Air raid in the middle, buffet afterwards, breakfast for sixteen,
the Karam Palace became very grand, almost too grand I'm afraid.
The Choremis, the Benachis, the Casullis, the Salvagos and others
rushing about like mad, celebrating in Pastroudis, dead with Cavafy.

The Karam Palace became very grand, almost too grand I'm afraid,
the glamorous women of Alexandria founded the best reference library.
Rushing about like mad, celebrating in Pastroudis, dead with Cavafy,
holding thirty percent of all the shares of banks and limited companies.

The glamorous women of Alexandria founded the best reference library,
during the summer the Burg el Arab served as base for Indian troops.
Holding thirty percent of all the shares of banks and limited companies,
the Britannia Club at 26 Rue Fuad, "proof of the British ability."

Judge

I am fallen into remembrance
of hot ghats, steam of bones, salt rituals
and pacific clouds, our fathers
dancing like bored wives to Tagore's
lowliest songs—they call to mind
a young girl's virginal hairbrushing,
her cat-moan in the middle of the night.
Radhabinod Pal, the valet in the dream
tells me, your ancestors were all of a mind:
you would be a flutter on the planet's butterfly
wings, sailing into anonymity as is your due
and of every copper-skinned boy
born to silent newspaper yogis.
You see how cities are laid to waste
in the blink of an eye, how millions of parchment
skins melt and tangle with the gross
anatomy scattered to the unknown wind,
wind that has fallen like night?
I am no metric of death.
I am a collapsed gyre of burial rites.
In the afternoons, forced to ride in the stately procession
—the victor's make-believe march to the courts—
I watch out of the Bentley's rain-streaked window
those lined up and waiting for justice,
and all I see on their elongated faces
(they are visitors from the planet of reality)
is the desire to write by fire,
fire that loves humanity like a mother
her only dead child—and I see that it is not true
that every soul has an epic to tell.

Passenger

electricity is paper and the eyes have it or not
the nyads of red desert-of-the-real manifestos

aching suburban chronicles congregated
one perfect story at a time refusing criticism

which is a young man's entitlement and fame
and all the poetry naysayers licking the boots

of the contemporary democrat's armor of grief
the widows anticipate how it will be to sing

alone or in company, how hard it is to pick up
how hard the noon doldrums among writers

of lyric prose slicing the muse's playful jugular
and bleeding through the crumbled stone houses

I found mcluhan in some kind of encyclopedic
or did I mean epigrammatic new millennium pose

even actresses write poetry after a discipline
even celebrities think it's all too easy to vamp on

words and their wordy brain-stalled functions
death of the author notwithstanding or rather

withstanding theory's infected lance and living
free like hallucinations dying of structure

elm

the tree bled, rivers of red, my things
pants and whole marmorials of insects—
oh gods of literature, ant-sized, riff
off this atmosphere of taut wisdom
how their planet's ache is off by zero
centuries in silent mode, i recall tiny
tiny the crushed vanquished bulldozed
elm fed on sixty years of fire under
the earth, moist as calculus, bones
wiggled like my toes like phantom
branches sitting on the arse of the
urban lubber like Pope something
or other i don't know, x is right? why
this soupbowl from ecosystem, ugly
nights, ugly "there's nothing i can do,
sorry, I've decided already, the tree
has to come down, people's sewage
is blocked, the roots are clogging
the pipes," i know that's not true,
but arses have to be wiped on time,
sweet pink arses smooth as perrier,
next morning i talk to my clueless
squirrels in the voice of a mellow
pumpkin, they've reduced me to a
head-banging positron in my own
home, i said to my wishful e. e.
i said 40 ft. over my naked roof
I said violence is what separates us

Ploughman

Ploughman, pygmy, peekaboo board of propertied
quaestors retreading the textures of deadline polls:

the death toll is a penalty of chalk stone, chagrin
among blushing witches, the rude autonomasia of

robust quiverfuls aching with positive vexillology.
The wave along the water main—your watchman

couch, coudé comporting with the beneficiaries of
lucent passwords—reflects percussion at the antic

refineries of slot-machine reproduction. The slit
along the chapbook chapel of ease, charity to new-

borns, is a moorland month of montane similitude,
and the medals like spirographs, tailpieces to death

that occurs like metal, or a fine-haired roof, back of
the bicycle, declining like the blown water-wheel.

The Singing Heralds of My Partner's Death

Something to fabulate the Febry Perot interferometer:
the eye socket spliced into the teeth of fabliaux where
what the eye doesn't see, the heart doesn't grieve over.
Honey, I am a locust to honors mushrooming around
the honnête homme I began to be as the cuatros flew
against nonadhesive snuff. Your dismembered snow-
plow, unpacked like the demiurges of Della Cruscan,
is dazzled by the daylong day of judgment: culminant
Dead Sea, quim fired in Cuba libre, the fake quietude
of the true-blue Trotsky you never were. I buttonhole
butterfly revolutions in the garden of bygones. I pass
the birth of venus under the bodhi tree, capitalism's
last schizophrenic schlump, seeing through your suff-
ragette odors, which then as now argue a theory of
views of vigilance, alarm bells at graduate exequies.

Notes

"Gertrude Stein" is made up of fragments from Gertrude Stein's *Tender Buttons* and John Malcolm Brinnin's *The Third Rose: Gertrude Stein and Her World* (Addison-Wesley, 1987).

"Poets" borrows from lines by Ron Silliman's *Demo to Ink* (Chax Press, 1992, p. 67), H.D.'s "A Dead Priestess Speaks" (*Collected Poems*, p. 369), William Wordsworth's "She dwelt among the untrodden ways," (*Lyrical Ballads*, ed. Michael Mason, p. 245), Martial's Ep. 5.37, "Of the Virgin Erotion" (*Martial in English*, ed. J. P. Sullivan and A. J. Boyle), and Antonin Artaud's "Cry" (*Selected Writings*, ed. Susan Sontag, 1976, p. 37).

"E. M. Forster in Alexandria" is adapted from Gareth L. Steen, ed., *Alexandria: the Site & the History* (NYU, 1993), Michael Haag's *Alexandria: City of Memory* (Yale, 2004), Mary Lago and P. N. Furbank, eds., *Selected Letters of E. M. Forster*, vol. 1, 1879-1920 (Harvard, 1983), Justin Pollard and Howard Reid's *The Rise and Fall of Alexandria* (Viking, 2006), Laura Foreman's *Alexander the Conqueror: The Epic Story of the Warrior King* (De Capo, 2004), Francis King's *E. M. Forster and His World* (Thames and Hudson, 1978), Michael Haag's *Alexandria Illustrated* (American University in Cairo, 2004), and P. N. Furbank's *E. M. Forster: A Life, Polycrates's Ring, 1914-1970*, vol. 2 (Secker & Warburg, 1978).

"Controlled Demolition" consists of fragments from David Harvey's *Rebel Cities: From the Right to the City to the Urban Revolution* (Verso, 2012), Don DeLillo's *Cosmopolis* (Scribner, 2003), and Slavoj Žižek's *Less Than Nothing: Hegel and the Shadow of Dialectical Materialism* (Verso, 2012).

"Alexandria in World War II" borrows from pgs. 182 and 183 of Michael Haag's *Alexandria: City of Memory* (Yale, 2004).

"Confessions" borrows from Jean-Jacques Rousseau's *Confessions*.

"Without Which He Would Not Have Written His Best Poems" is composed of alternating excerpts from Judy Bastyra and Nitya Lacroix's *The Good Sex Bible: How to Make Love* (Hermes House, 2010) and *The Letters of T.S. Eliot, Volume 3: 1926-1927* (Yale, 2012).

"The Beats" is adapted from John Tytell's *Paradise Outlaws: Remembering the Beats* (Morrow, 1999).

"Enemies in Bed" is made up of alternating borrowings from David Lehman's *The Last Avant-Garde: The Making of the New York School of Poets* (Doubleday, 1998) and Kenneth Koch's *Collected Poems* (Knopf, 2005).

"Oscar Wilde" is adapted from Stephen Calloway and David Colvin's *The Exquisite Life of Oscar Wilde* (Orion Books, 1997).

"Mountolive" is taken from Lawrence Durrell's novel of the same title in *The Alexandria Quartet*.

"Loneliness" is google scuplted.

"Averroes," "The Habit of Novel Reading," and **"Recluse"** are found poems.

Anis Shivani is the author of several critically acclaimed books of fiction, poetry, and criticism, including *Anatolia and Other Stories (*2009), *Against the Workshop: Provocations, Polemics, Controversies* (2011), *The Fifth Lash and Other Stories* (2012), *My Tranquil War and Other Poems* (2012), and *Karachi Raj: A Novel* (2015). Both *Anatolia and Other Stories* and *The Fifth Lash and Other Stories* were longlisted for the Frank O'Connor international short story award. Forthcoming books include *Soraya: Sonnets* and *Literature in an Age of Globalization*. Books in progress or recently finished include *Death is a Festival: Poems*, *Plastic Realism: Neoliberalism in Recent American Fiction*, and the novels *A History of the Cat in Nine Chapters or Less*, *Abruzzi, 1936*, and *An Idiot's Guide to America*. Anis's work appears in the *Yale Review*, *Georgia Review, Boston Review, Iowa Review, Threepenny Review, Michigan Quarterly Review, Antioch Review, Southwest Review, Prairie Schooner, AGNI, Fence, Epoch, Boulevard, Pleiades, Denver Quarterly, Verse, Colorado Review, Quarterly West, New Letters, Subtropics, Times Literary Supplement, London Magazine, Meanjin, Fiddlehead*, and other leading literary journals. Anis is a member of the National Book Critics Circle, and his reviews appear widely in newspapers and magazines such as the *Huffington Post, Daily Beast, In These Times, Texas Observer, San Francisco Chronicle, Boston Globe, Austin American-Statesman, Kansas City Star, Pittsburgh Post-Gazette, St. Petersburg Times, Charlotte Observer*, and many other outlets. Anis is the winner of a 2012 Pushcart Prize, was educated at Harvard College, and lives in Houston, Texas.

Made in the USA
San Bernardino, CA
16 April 2017